SELAH 2

... pause and think on purpose!

Selah 2 ... pause and think on purpose!
First published July 2007

Houston, Brian
ISBN 09752060 3 6

Scripture quotations used in this book are from the following sources
and used with permission:
New King James Version (NKJV). Copyright © 1982, 1992 by Thomas
Nelson, Inc. Used by permission. All rights reserved.
Amplified Bible (AMP). Old Testament Copyright © 1965, 1987 by the
Zondervan Corporation. New Testament copyright © 1958, 1987 by
the Lockman Foundation. Used by permission.
New International Version (NIV). Copyright © 1973,1978, 1984
International Bible Society. All rights reserved throughout the world.
Used by permission of International Bible Society.
The Message by Eugene H. Peterson, copyright © 1993,1994, 1995,
1996, 2000, 2001, 2002. Used by permission of NavPress Publishing
Group. All rights reserved.

Bold emphasis in certain scriptures are the author's own.

Photographs by Bobbie Houston, Brian Houston, Darren Kitto,
Tim Skinner, David Anderson, and others.

Layout and design by Daryl-Anne Le Roux.

Printed by Pegasus Printing, Rosebery NSW Australia.

Published by Leadership Ministries Inc.
www. leadershipministries.com.au

SELAH

... pause and think on purpose!

BRIAN HOUSTON

pur·pose

[noun] 1. the reason for which something is done or for which it exists. 2. resolve or determination

Pause and think on purpose ...

People can endlessly ponder on the meaning of life, but when they discover the Cause of Christ, they begin to live a life of meaning.

We're not on earth to mark time, we're here to make a difference. To live a life of purpose is to live a life that goes beyond yourself.

Many centuries ago, King Solomon wrote of God, "He also has planted eternity in men's hearts and minds [**a divinely implanted sense of a purpose** working through the ages which nothing under the sun but God alone can satisfy]." (Ecclesiastes 3:11 AMP)

There's a 'divinely implanted sense of a purpose' in all of us. I pray the thoughts in this book will encourage you to discover your purpose, and inspire you to outwork it in all that you do.

The secret to
living a life of PURPOSE is

living for something BIGGER
than yourself.

We can't do everything

but we must DO SOMETHING.

'What does the Lord require of you but to do justly, to love mercy, and to walk humbly with your God?' [Micah 6:8]

When God gives you

a sense of PURPOSE,

you're ruined for anything else.

SALVATION is more than an insurance policy against hell.

Don't just live saved – live CALLED.

'[God] has saved us and called us with a holy calling...' [2 Timothy 1:9]

helping others

because we care

The best way to find
fulfilment in life
is by helping
OTHERS...

BECAUSE WE CAN.

PURPOSE changes
your mind about
what's a **luxury** and
what's a **necessity**.

I can't afford a lack of discipline (Proverbs 5:23)

I can't afford a lack of judgement (Proverbs 9:4)

I can't afford a lack of direction (Proverbs 11:14)

I can't afford a lack of counsel (Proverbs 15:22)

I can't afford a lack of resource (Proverbs 22:27)

I can't afford a lack of knowledge (Hosea 4:6)

We can live as **small** as
our narrow thinking…

or as **BIG** as our open hearts.

When our HEARTS are open,

our HANDS are open.

'You shall open your hand wide to your brother, to your poor and needy in your land.' [Deuteronomy 15:11]

True justice may start with a **hand out**, but it's committed to a **hand up**.

A vision has options

but a CAUSE leaves you no choice.

'For Christ's love compels us.' [2 Corinthians 5:14 NIV]

Bobbie at the genocide memorial in Kigali, Rwanda.

Justice can't be reduced to a project, a protest or a crusade.

Justice is a HEART.

SIGNIFICANCE
is not found in
the **advancement of self**...

but in your **impact on others**.

A **self-made man** has seriously limited his life.

Self can't take you where **GOD** intends you to go.

The more you get to **know** GOD,

the more you realise there is to
KNOW.

'Oh, the depth of the riches both of the wisdom and knowledge of God!
How unsearchable are His judgments and His ways past finding out!'
[Romans 11:33]

Some people have just enough religion to HATE

but not enough
religion to LOVE.

Your ACCENT won't
make you a foreigner here...

but your ATTITUDE might!

[Spoken to the students at Hillsong International Leadership College during orientation.]

The best way to fulfil what's in your HEART

is to faithfully use what's in
your HAND.

Do you see WORK as

a means to an **end**

or a means to a **beginning**?

Achievement, accomplishment and purpose all begin with hard work.

A good leader will LABOUR for

the **prosperity** of another.

It's the will of God for us to **leave room** in our lives to invest in others.

'When you reap the harvest of your land, do not reap to the very edges of your field.' [Leviticus 19:9 NIV]

Your life is not meant to be a
LIST of competing priorities:

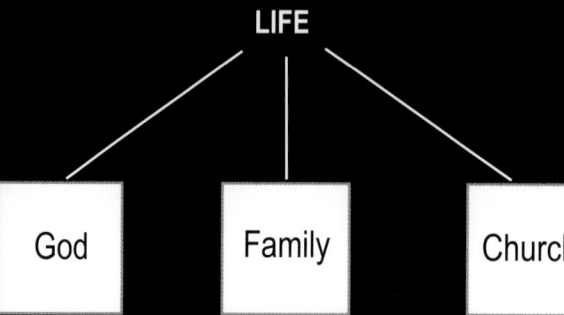

Simplify your life by
de-compartmentalising.

FULFILL YOUR PURPOSE BY
LOVING WHAT
GOD LOVES...

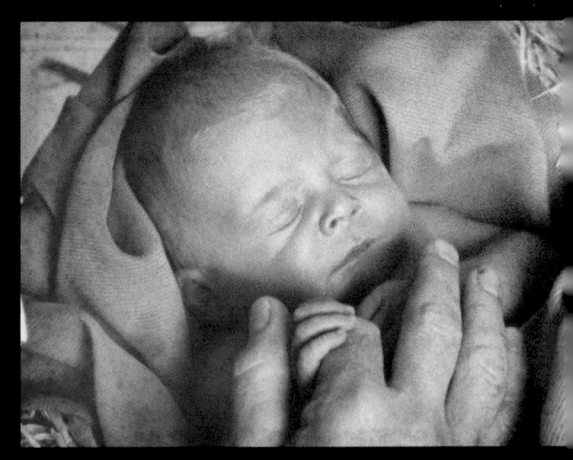

HIS SON

suddenly a great company of the HEAVENLY HOST appeared praising GOD and saying "GLORY TO GOD in the highest and on earth, peace to men on whom His favour rests."

Luke 2:13-14

JESUS...

CHURCH...

...HUMANITY.

You can't determine
what **CONFRONTS** you in life

but you **can** determine

what **FOLLOWS** you.

'Surely goodness and mercy shall follow me all the days of my life.' [Psalm 23:6]

MAKING

a commitment is easy,

but fruitfulness is found in its
KEEPING.

Don't want
what somebody else has got

if you're not prepared to
pay the price they've paid.

My loyalty to the FUTURE

will always exceed

my loyalty to the PAST.

Are you leaving a LEGACY for the next generation

or **squandering** the blessing of past generations?

The blessing of the
next **GENERATION**
should make the success of our

generation look small.

[Psalm 145:4]

GOD is in
the untried,
the unproven
and the unknown.

You don't gain influence by holding on to the model of our fathers or by doing what's already been done.

You can't **serve** history if

you want to **MAKE** history.

History is a helpful teacher but a terrible master.

TEXTBOOKS don't build churches.

Commit to building **people** and you can build a great **church**.

CREATIVITY
lies in the unestablished.

My initial sketches of the Hillsong Chapel on a napkin.

Be the kind of person that inspires a

'**CAN DO**' spirit in others.

Hillsong Conference volunteers, 2006

A **volunteer spirit** is the sign of a healthy church.

'Your people shall be volunteers in the day of your power.' [Psalm 110:3]

LOYALTY is active, not passive.

It should be obvious.

Demonstrate it.
Declare it.
Speak it.
Pledge it.

Are you living at the level of your **problem**

or at the level of your **answer**?

The **GRACE** of God
is a perfect fit
for your calling.

لأن الناموس بموسى أعطي
أما النعمة والحق
فبيسوع المسيح صارا.   يوا:١٧

For while the law was given through
Moses;
grace and truth came through
Jesus Christ.   JOHN 1:17

Wall plaque at Mount Nebo, Jordan

RELEVANCE

[to be useful and suitable to a purpose]

It's the **message** that's sacred,

not the **method**.

Are you happy in your relationships?

The only thing common to all of your relationships...

is YOU!

If you keep the people around you **small**,

you consign yourself to living in
a smaller world.

'Those who are planted in the House of the Lord shall flourish.' [Psalm 92:13]

The **smaller** the man on the inside

the **BIGGER** the opinion.

YOU may have a **reason** for staying the way you are

but GOD has a **reason** for you becoming all you CAN be.

We need to be accountable for what's going on INTERNALLY

so we can be honest EXTERNALLY.

There are three ways to learn in life:

1. The easy way

– from other people's mistakes.

2. The hard way

– from our own mistakes.

3. The tragic way

– when we don't learn from either.

The weight of religion holds good men **down**

but the Gospel of Jesus lifts the downtrodden **up**.

'He raises the poor out of the dust, and lifts the needy out of the ash heap.' [Psalm 113:7]

There's no such thing as a 'prosperity gospel'.

There's only ONE Gospel – the Gospel of Jesus Christ!

Practice generosity everywhere!

'A generous man devises generous things.' [Isaiah 32:8]

When you have PURPOSE
in your heart...

you'll have PURPOSE
in your mouth.

'Out of the abundance of the heart the mouth speaks.' [Luke 6:45]

Are all the wrong **moments**
in your life defining your **YEARS**...

or will consistency through the **YEARS** build incredible **moments**?

If you want to last the distance,

learn to **ENJOY** the journey.

The key to fulfilling a life of purpose:

Just keep turning up!

For more information on resources by Brian Houston:
www.leadershipministries.com.au